THE LIE ABOUT THE WEST

By the same author
THE WAR ON LAND, 1914–1918
THE LIE ABOUT THE WAR
AN INTRODUCTION TO THE HISTORY OF ENGLAND
(From the earliest times to 1204)
ENGLAND—PAST, PRESENT, AND FUTURE
ETC.

THE LIE ABOUT
THE WEST

*A response to
Professor Toynbee's challenge*

BY DOUGLAS JERROLD

Sheed and Ward • New York • 1954

15189

A part of this book was printed in the
Sewanee Review

THE LIE ABOUT THE WEST

PROFESSOR ARNOLD TOYNBEE has expounded in his massive work *A Study of History* his doctrine of challenge and response as the key to the correct understanding of the historical process. In his latest book, *The World and the West*,[1] he sets out to apply his theories to the present world situation, which he sees, broadly, as arising from the 'response' of the world to the persistent and aggressive challenge of 'the West.' The outcome of this challenge he foretells, by analogy, from the outcome of the 'response' of the world to the 'challenge' of the Greeks and Romans.

At the time of the break-up of the Roman Empire the 'disillusioned Greek and Roman dominant

[1] Oxford University Press, New York, 1953.

minority, was, in fact, suffering from the same spiritual starvation as the majority of contemporary mankind. . . . After the Greeks and Romans had conquered the world by force of arms, the world took its conquerors captive by converting them to new religions which addressed their message to all human souls, without discriminating between rulers and subjects or between Greeks, orientals, and barbarians. Is something like this historic denouement of the Graeco-Roman story going to be written into the unfinished history of the world's encounter with the West?'

Since his book was published, the Professor has been good enough to explain the meaning of this passage. 'The West and the world,' he thinks,[1] are going to 'become converted to an Oriental religion coming neither from Russia nor from the West. I guess that this will be the Christian religion that came to the Greeks and Romans from Palestine with one of two elements in traditional Christianity discarded and replaced by a new element from India. I expect and hope that this avatar of Christianity will include the vision of God as being Love.

[1] Letter in the London *Times Literary Supplement* for April 16th, 1954.

2

But I also expect and hope that it will discard the other traditional Christian vision of God as being a jealous god, and that it will reject the self-glorification of this jealous god's "Chosen People" as being unique. This is where India comes in, with her belief (complementary to the vision of God as Love) that there may be more than one illuminating and saving approach to the mystery of the universe.' In his letter in which all this (of which no word is contained in his book on *The World and the West*) is explained, Professor Toynbee evidently thinks that his gloss on his earlier broadcast message will be reassuring at least to the West. It does, indeed, show that he neither greatly expects nor at all desires the triumph of Communism, as some of his readers wrongly thought, but it is hardly reassuring, nonetheless, to the great Christian majority in the West, who are asked to expect a new dispensation which involves their admission that the religion which they have hitherto confessed is compounded of a variety of errors.

The importance of *The World and the West* lies not only in its conclusions (which, if they be well founded, are equally ominous for the future of Christianity and of liberal humanism), but in its provenance. Professor Toynbee has a high reputation on both sides of the Atlantic. He has been hitherto widely regarded as representative of liberal opinion in the English-speaking world, and *The World and the West* is a reprint of his Reith Lectures, the annual series sponsored by the British Broadcasting Corporation. Exceptional importance attaches to these lectures. Although the Corporation cannot fairly be presumed to agree with all the views expressed, the choice of the lecturer is certainly intended to indicate that his views merit particular consideration. These lectures provide, in fact, the only occasion when the Corporation allows the exposition at full length, and with no right of reply from anyone, of a considered view on world affairs: they have, therefore, at least a semi-official character.

Earl Russell, in the Reith Lectures for 1951, was the first to strike a note of pessimism. He was disposed to accept little from the past, although he was prepared to concede nothing to Communism. In *The World and the West* pessimism as to the future of Christian civilization is carried to the point where listeners are, as it seems to me, urged to leave the sinking ship, to see almost every other

4

point of view except the Christian's, and to meet our enemies in the gates before they storm the citadel.

Let it be said at once that Professor Toynbee's message is not crystal clear. It is indeed certain that what the Professor sees as desirable is a philosophic, not a political, capitulation. It is, however, impossible not to feel that his purpose is to instil a doubt not only as to the probable efficacy of any active defence of Western values as understood to-day, but as to the survival at the heart of our civilization of values worth defending at all costs and to the end.

His argument is indeed even more surprising for its omissions than for its statements. To him Western civilization has degenerated into technology, applied to worthless purposes by men without a mission or a creed. That which has appeared to countless millions of our race as a civilizing process wherein man has been awakened to the knowledge of God, and through that knowledge, to the understanding of his own potentialities and a consciousness of his responsibilities, which has made man at once a morally responsible being and a free moral agent, is represented in this book as nothing

more than the march of armies trampling ruthlessly
on the hopes and aspirations of mankind. His story
is the story of wars waged in the interests of dominant minorities. Such august concepts as the rule
of law, the rights of conscience, the right of free
speech and free association, the right to life, liberty,
and the pursuit of happiness, the right, sacred above
all other rights, of men to save their souls by ful-
filling the purpose of their being as free moral
agents in correspondence with Divine Grace: none
of these supremely important things which have
been won for millions of men through the slow,
painful, and laborious processes of Western civilization finds a direct mention in this book. We do
find, however, one indirect but vitally significant
reference to all these things in the statement that
'the falsity of our belief in our own unique value
does not become apparent to us. . . . We westerners
being human are inclined to feel that what we have
done to the world within the last few centuries is
something unprecedented. An effective cure for this
Western illusion of ours is to glance back at what,
not so very long ago, was done to the world by the
Greeks and Romans. We shall see that they too
overran the world in their day and that they too

believed for a time that they were not as other men.'

It is tempting to ask whether it would be possible to condense more nonsense into fewer sentences. But professors do not consciously write nonsense. For Professor Toynbee the sentences given must have a meaning, and that meaning appears, at first sight, to be that Christianity is a false religion, for it is self-evident that if it be true it is unique; and secondly that those Western humanist liberal concepts which have derived from the fusion of the classical and the Christian cultures are not absolute values in the sense of being absolutely necessary to the good society, but are only relatively good in relation to our particular society, which is no better absolutely than any other. To that two things must be said. First, it is very wrong, in my submission, to base an argument on judgments so controversial without stating them explicitly. Secondly, it is equally wrong to place before a popular audience judgments of this order as if they were the accepted judgments of all competent scholars requiring no word of argument in their support. The one argument in which the Professor indulges, when he says that we can be quickly cured of our belief in the uniqueness of the Christian revelation, and the society to which it has given birth, by recalling that the Greeks and Romans also thought their society unique, is puerile. The facts, in the first place, are untrue, but if they were as stated, if there had been in fact nothing unique about Greek art, poetry, and philosophy, or about Roman law and government, which there manifestly was, the conclusion which the Professor draws from his alleged facts would not follow. The fact that some men have believed a lie does not prove that other men believing something quite different are equally mistaken.[1]

It is the Professor's conviction that Western values are not unique, nor of supreme importance, except maybe to ourselves, which inspires his argument. He asks us to look at it all from the other

---

[1] Professor Toynbee has subsequently explained (the *Times Literary Supplement,* April 30th) that, while he denies absolutely the 'uniqueness' of western Christian civilization, he does so mainly because we are all sinners. 'Christ's unique merits cannot be appropriated by any human being or by any institution.' I fail to see that this is relevant, even if it is true. No one has ever asserted that all men, or all institutions, in the West were superior to those in the East—merely that our society bears witness, however imperfectly, to certain truths, and derives such strength as it possesses from its fidelity to certain principles of social organization enjoined on it by the Christian religion in which it believes.

fellow's point of view. That is, of course, a salutary thing to do. It is unfortunately true that to the orthodox Hindu, to the Chinese, to the Moslems, many of us do not appear to-day in the guise of missionaries preaching a gospel of redemption, but as technologists offering only such salvation as may be won by sanitation. We cannot, the progressives appear to think, teach the Eastern peoples how to live, but we can teach them how not to be born. What the Professor fails to ask himself is by what right he misdescribes this jejune nihilism as the representative wisdom of the West; and by what right it can be represented, in particular, as characteristic of Christian civilization. We are asked to haul down the flag, to admit our errors, on the assumption that our flag is only an intellectualized version of the Jolly Roger, and our errors only the same errors as those of all other men worshipping false gods. The vaults of the bank of Christian civilization are only filled with counterfeit paper: what need then of the police? Let us fill them up instead with the more fashionable currency of the hour, and those who have put the new currency into circulation and depend on its repute will do the policing for us.

And if in this way we meet our enemies in the

gates and hand them the keys of the citadel, shall we not be able to preserve the appearance of independence, if not with credit at least without danger or effort?

If indeed we have nothing to defend, it were folly to waste time defending it. It is for this reason that it is imperative to examine the Professor's allegedly historical argument in detail, for it would indeed be a tragedy if we acted hastily on his assumptions and found out only too late that they were mistaken. If the Christian centuries, under the inspiration not only of the glory that was Greece and the grandeur that was Rome but of the teachings of Christ and His Church, have in fact done no more for the world, be it Western or Eastern, than slaughter and betray, then the sooner Christian civilization be merged in some conquering synthesis the better. But if it be otherwise, then we must face with courage and determination the enemy within our gates, or else we shall forfeit all hope of withstanding the formidable forces which threaten us from without.

THE Professor begins by explaining why he calls his book *The World and the West*. It is the West which is, and has been for many centuries, the aggressor. 'The World, not the West, is the party that, up to now, has had the significant experience. It has not been the West which has been hit by the world; it is the world that has been hit—and hit hard—by the West.' His first chapter deals with Russia, the victim of Western aggression for the last six centuries; his second chapter deals with the Moslem world, whose sufferings at our hands have been, according to Professor Toynbee, almost as cruel, although he accords the Moslems the credit for having 'liberated from a Christian-Graeco-Roman ascendancy a string of oriental countries—from Syria right across North

Africa to Spain—which had been under Greek or Roman rule for nearly a thousand years. . . . After that the Moslems went on to conquer by stages almost the whole of India, and their religion spread peacefully even further afield.'

It is desirable to interpose a word of explanation at this point. Words which mean one thing to us mean another to Professor Toynbee. The six centuries of Western aggression against Russia are in fact the six centuries which have witnessed the expansion of Russian dominion from the small land-locked state of Muscovy in the fourteenth century to the great empire which we now know—infinitely the largest continental empire known to history. The manifest encroachments of Russia on the territory of her neighbours since 1918 are only the continuation of a process which has been far more regular and continuous over a longer period, and far less often interrupted, than the expansion of any other state or people in the history of the world. As a matter of history as we, though not Professor Toynbee, understand it, this process has only once been strongly checked, in 1918, when the sovereignty over the lands of the Poles, Finns, Esthonians, Lithuanians, and Latvians was temporarily restored to those unfortunate peoples. It need hardly be added that this retrograde step was the result, according to the Professor, of Western aggression.

As for the Moslem and the Christian-Graeco-Roman dominion for a thousand years over North Africa and Spain, it is news indeed that North Africa and Spain are oriental countries, and that liberal progressives regard the restoration of the *status quo* of a thousand years ago as a legitimate and, indeed, praiseworthy act of liberation. If Hitler had succeeded in conquering England, would the Professor have regarded it as an act of liberation from the dominance of the Norman minority; or would he have preferred to see Mussolini liberating our unfortunate islanders from the Anglo-Saxon dominance resulting from their aggression against Roman rule in the fourth century? And since when, we may ask, has it been considered logical in academic circles to equate conversion by conquest with the peaceful spread of religion? The Professor is far too good a writer of the English language to have written that the Moslem religion 'spread peacefully even further afield' unless he meant that it was a process already begun which was continued. After that it will hardly surprise the reader to learn that India, described in chapter two as conquered by the Moslems, appears in the third chapter not as a country liberated by the West from Moslem dominance, but as a victim of Western aggression. The fourth chapter deals with China and Japan, two unconquered countries which have nevertheless suffered economic and religious aggression from the ruthless westerners. Having surveyed the stricken fields of Western aggression, the Professor turns in his fifth chapter to the lesson to be learnt from this sad story—and the lesson is this, 'that a society which is under fire from the radiation of a more potent foreign culture must either master this foreign way of life or perish.' The military metaphor is characteristic of the Professor's approach. All cultures are to him warring against each other; the impact of one on another is hostile, dangerous, and painful. Furthermore, 'the penetrative power of a strand of cultural radiation is usually in inverse ratio to this strand's cultural value. A trivial strand arouses less resistance in the assaulted body social than is aroused by a crucial strand' and 'the very process of diffraction, which is the essence of the game (of cultural intercourse),

14

threatens to poison the life of the society whose body social is being penetrated.'

The implications of this argument are what concern us here. If you take one element, for the sake of argument technology or science, from a foreign culture and try to graft it on to your own culture, you will kill that culture at its roots. The virtues of the peasant society wither in the presence of the huckster; the pagan virtues perish in the presence of the missionary; the martial virtues perish in the presence of the priest. Unless, therefore, you absorb the whole of an alien culture, the result of contact with it, if it be more potent, will be to destroy the defence of your own culture and lead to its annihilation.

The Professor's argument here, albeit deriving from a series of far-fetched and theoretically indefensible analogies, is supported by a number of familiar and persuasive examples of the practical consequences of the partial westernization of oriental and African societies. The argument has force and can probably be regarded as valid within the relatively narrow limits applicable to all historical generalization. The impartial and unlearned reader will probably say, and will possibly be right to say:

'The Professor certainly has something here.' But the crux lies in the implication, for the argument is addressed to the fate of cultures confronted with another culture more potent, more 'radioactive,' more dominating, and with greater penetrative power than they themselves possess. And when the Professor concludes by asking us to see how the Graeco-Roman world, at its nadir, fared in this situation and to learn our lessons from that story, it is once again evident that he is assuming the relative impotence and worthlessness of our own contemporary Western Christian civilization.

By what canon of historical scholarship is it possible to make such an assumption without any reference to institutional Christianity; without any characterization of the civilization built upon the Christian foundation; and without even calling attention to the fundamental differences in terms of moral and intellectual values (be they for better or worse makes no difference to this point) between the contemporary Christian and non-Christian civilizations—differences never more plainly visible to the world than they are to-day? How is it possible to make this assumption as regards the Western world of our day without discussing and evaluating the very distinct and surely dynamic culture of the North American continent, and in particular of the United States, to-day the dominant Western power, but nowhere mentioned in this book? These must surely be subjects for legitimate criticism.

Professor Toynbee attempts to anticipate this last criticism with the glib statement that the Russians 'do not draw fine distinctions between different hordes of Franks.' To the Russians (as also to the Asians and Africans) we are all Franks anyhow! But will this really do? If we are using the term 'the West' as synonymous with a culture, we must use it only of that geographical area which belongs to that culture. We cannot pick and choose among the peoples and their leaders and treat as representative westerners only those who march east. The first encounter between the 'West' and the 'world' to which our attention is drawn is the campaign of Alexander the Great, when there was no high civilization at all in the Western world as the term would be used to-day. In what sense was the West as we know it to-day a party to the wars of the third century B.C.? We may, perhaps, concede to Professor Toynbee the identification of the Roman Empire at its zenith with the West as it is

known to history, because it was during the first
centuries of the Roman Empire that the classical
culture and the Christian religion, the twin founda-
tions of our civilization, took firm root in Western
Europe. We cannot, however, agree with his description of the age-long struggle in the central
European plain between the Germans and the successive waves of invaders from the east as a series
of aggressions by the Western world, which, in fact,
stood consistently aloof from this central European
struggle. The European frontiers of the old Roman
Empire, as of the western world to-day, were the
Rhine and the Danube. The struggles in central
Europe, so far from being the symptoms of Western
aggression, enabled the Christian heirs of the old
Roman civilization behind these frontiers to develop
(once they had absorbed the Viking invaders) a
high civilization of their own, based on the national
state in combination (or sometimes in conflict) with
a supernational Church. Is it not precisely to that
separation of Church and State, and that reaction
from the old idea of a universal secular sovereignty,
that the West owes its peculiar character and qualities? To identify the West with every tyrant, from
Alexander to Hitler, who has marched eastward

and to ignore the clear facts that they did not come from the West in any historically valid sense, and that they were, one and all, in revolt against the specifically Western values, is to remove almost all meaning from the term 'Western,' except as a quality to be predicated of every military adventurer, wherever he comes from, and whatever he believes in, who marches east.

Here again we have, indeed, the same underlying assumption that what we call 'Western values' are in fact of no special significance culturally, politically, or socially. How otherwise could Professor Toynbee write in his third chapter that from a point of view which 'takes in the whole of mankind, the diverse Moslem and Christian variations on a common Graeco-Jewish way of life fade almost out of view. When we contrast our Moslem-Christian way of life as a whole with the Hindu way or with the Far Eastern, the differences, inside our Moslem-Christian family, between Eastern Orthodox Christendom and Western Christendom, or between either of these Christendoms and Islam, almost cease to be visible.'

In other words, the once generally accepted view that Western Christian civilization is profoundly different in its character, and in the values which it asserts, from any other civilization, has no validity. Otherwise it would be nonsensical for the Professor to adopt a viewpoint so remote that the differences, for all practical purposes, disappear.

What Professor Toynbee has, in fact, attempted to do in this book is to make such a reassessment of the history of the West over the last two thousand years as shall lead his readers to the conclusion that the specifically Western character in our society is its continuous military and cultural aggression; that such good qualities and principles as it possesses are really common to Moslems and to Christians, to Communist and to individualist communities; and that we can no longer usefully and hopefully assert the individuality or essentiality of our values and institutions, or claim to preserve them, in the face of a world which is increasingly resentful of them. Fundamental changes, we are to infer, in the structure and character of our society, and in the nature of our fundamental beliefs, are not only long overdue but inevitable, as part of an historical process which is largely predetermined by the nature of men and things. It is this thesis that gives great importance to this reprint of the Reith Lectures,

coming to us as they do in the first place from a
quasi-governmental institution, and from the lips of
a highly representative figure in our public life, at a
moment when political leaders of the Western communities are trying to energize their peoples for the
defence of the Western way of life against the progressive incursions of an alien and illiberal tyranny.

THE argument from history against the Christian claims, and against the principles of social life and organization to which Christian belief has given rise, has itself a long history. It has seldom, however, been applied so confidently and so provocatively as it is by Professor Toynbee, nor have we ever been asked to accept from it such drastic conclusions. Do the Professor's conclusions proceed from the facts of history? How far, on the contrary, should they be regarded as an eleventh-hour effort to salvage the materialist case against the Christian conception of society from the criticisms which have overtaken its earlier presentations?

Our contemporary civilization, which is to-day threatened, derives its values and its institutions in part from Greece and Rome and, as to the more important part, from Christianity (whether Christianity be a true or a false religion that statement remains historically true). It is usual to say that Western civilization, from the rise of the Greek city state to the present day, shows one continuous process of development, to which a decisive turn was given by the conversion of the West to Christianity between the first and the seventh centuries A.D. It is the belief of the Western world to-day that in the process man has been led to greater heights of achievement, spiritual, intellectual, and material, than in any other civilization; and that, therefore, the basic institutions of our world and the basic rights of all men and women which those institutions sustain—the free Church, the free family, the independent State, and the right of each and all, irrespective of race, class, or colour, to freedom of conscience and freedom of thought—must at all costs, and if necessary at the cost of our own lives, be preserved.

It is nothing new in modern times that this view should be challenged by historians. For many centuries, it is true, the historical argument about the civilization of the West was concerned almost exclusively with the nature and extent of the papal prerogatives and with the relations of the Church and the secular power. When, however, in the seventeenth and eighteenth centuries, it became fashionable to speculate about the nature and origins of human society, the philosophers tended to find in history the story of progressive improvement wherever conditions were favourable to free change, and of stagnation only where authority held sway. When we remember that the eighteenth-century philosophers of the so-called 'Enlightenment' found their opportunity for popularizing their revolutionary secularist doctrines in the misuse of power by the despotisms of the *ancien régime,* this was perhaps to be expected. Being totally ignorant of almost all that is now known, from archaeology and anthropology, of the nature of primitive societies and of the archaic civilizations, the various guesses of the philosophers about the simple virtue and natural wisdom of our primitive ancestors seemed reasonable enough: having assumed an Arcadian past they then had to find reasons for an extremely murky present, and found them almost inevitably, given their initial guesses, in the baneful influence of the two institutions—Church and State—which,

24

between them, seemed chiefly to have moulded the destinies of men.

These ingenious, and quite unhistorical, theories proved at once acceptable to all who for any reason were hostile to the Christian religion and to the existing secular order; the rift between historical speculation and Christian orthodoxy grew wider when the earlier theories of evolution seemed to give scientific support to the belief in an inherent tendency to progress. The discoveries which we owe to the more modern sciences of archaeology and anthropology, however, render the simple theories of the Enlightenment, as far as they relate to progress and to man's natural wisdom and virtue, as untenable to-day by atheists as by Christians.

From the beginnings of what is now called pre-history to the classical civilization, the history of man is now known to be the history not of a slow and laborious ascent, but of successive civilizations rising, maturing, and declining. We can trace, for instance, the growth, use, and decline of art in the first historical period of Egypt, which ended with the Second Dynasty; again in the age of the pyramid builders, from the end of the Third Dynasty to the Sixth; again in the Middle Period from the

Ninth Dynasty to the Hyksos invasion; and again in the Hyksos period and in the time of the New Kingdom, ending in the Twentieth Dynasty. A similar cycle, roughly contemporaneous, can be accurately traced in the Early Minoan, the Middle Minoan, and the Mycenaean cultures. The same cycle of civilizations can be traced in China, with approximately the same intervals (a thousand years) between them. We also know that the rise of the new civilization, in every known case down to our own, has been associated with a new admixture of races. Wherever the record is complete, the development of the arts and sciences seems to have followed a roughly uniform course, beginning with architecture and sculpture, followed by painting and literature, and ending with an age of applied art and mathematics.

These facts soon gave rise to an imposing edifice of speculation. The first reaction of the frightened believers in the theory of a natural progress, which by the end of the nineteenth century had come to be generally accepted by all except the believers in original sin, was an ingenious use of the new chronology which had been disclosed by scientific inquiry into prehistory. Very well, the believers in

26

automatic progress said in effect, it is accepted that man's progress has been more chequered than we had thought, but the fact of progress remains. We must not focus our eyes on the last ten thousand years of history: man has been roaming the globe for half a million years, or even, as some think, for a million years or more: seen in perspective, the set-backs have occupied but a moment of time in the vast process from the first living cell to the twentieth-century professor.

The fallacy involved here has proved, nevertheless, too glaring to satisfy the disquiet of the progressives, particularly in the light of the shattering events of the last half-century. The length of the pre-cultural stage of man's history no more reduces the validity of judgments about civilization based on the history of civilized societies than modern discoveries about the size of the universe reduce the importance of man. The importance alike of history and of man is qualitative, not quantitative. The problem for historical inquiry is not the length of pre-cultural history but the facts of cultural history.

Sir Flinders Petrie in 1911 drew attention to the curiously repetitive pattern shown by the civilizations of the West, the classical civilization, the late

Egyptian (Theban) civilization, the Egyptian Middle Kingdom, and the Egypt of the pyramids.[1]

His small book excited little attention, and the cyclical theory of history only achieved world-wide notoriety with the publication of Oswald Spengler's *Decline of the West*. This work was for long despised by the English-speaking world on both sides of the Atlantic. Firstly, Spengler had the misfortune to be a German and was therefore soon suspected

---

[1] Sir Flinders Petrie gives the following approximate dates for the optimum period of the different phases of civilization in (A) the western European cycle, (B) the classical period, (C) the late Egyptian (Theban) civilization, (D) the Egyptian Middle Kingdom, and (E) the Egypt of the pyramids. His chronology for the last two periods gives a longer period to these civilizations than that generally adopted. He regards each civilization as 'established' when the climax is reached in the development of sculpture, and the figures below show the interval elapsing between the climax of sculpture and the climax of the other phases of civilization.

Date of establishment of civilization:

	A	B	C	D	E
	AD 1240	450 BC	1550 BC	3450 BC	4750 BC
Sculpture	—	—	—	—	—
Painting	160	100	80	50	50 (?)
Literature	360	200	200	130	—
Mechanics	550	450	270	180	100 (?)
Science	650	600	—	—	—
Wealth	650	650	370	200	—

28

of anti-democratic sympathies. Secondly, and more justifiably, Spengler, who was not a professional historian, was criticized as a dangerously speculative amateur. Sir Flinders Petrie, trained by long years of research in the discipline of limiting his conclusions to those deducible from the evidence he could cite, contented himself with announcing the parallelisms. He did not attempt to explain them. Spengler went further and fared worse in the process. Nevertheless, for all its faults, and indeed in some cases its positive absurdities, *The Decline of the West* marks a turning-point in historical speculation. It asked a new question and gave to contemporary history a new context. What we must all study to-day is not the law which governs the progress of societies, but that which appears to dictate their decline. Whatever we think of the Spengler synthesis, the facts synthesized remain.

The empiricists, like H. A. L. Fisher, who looked at the world of the twenties with profound disquiet, were content to say that, desperate though the outlook was, they were unable to detect any pattern in history which gave ground for rational pessimism. Fisher saw only too clearly the reasons for the world's tragedy. He could see no reason why these reasons should recur. He had no faith in God, but he retained a diminished but still firm faith in man's capacity to save himself, at least from the worst consequences of his follies and his crimes.

With no more comfort than could be derived from this scholarly, humanistic, but negative answer, which was the best that liberal positivism could offer to the new riddle, intellectuals throughout Europe began to move from the centre and to group themselves on the right or the left. Could the Christians after all be right in thinking that freedom was only possible to man within a closed moral system buttressed by institutions designed to fortify and stimulate the natural virtues; or, branching off from Hegel, were we forced to accept the attractively simple conclusions of dialectical materialism? In the language of the headlines, was the choice really between the Christian and Marxist philosophies of history, and must we in either case believe to be saved? Was there no place for a cultivated scepticism in the brave new world?

The progressive hardening of European opinion on the right and on the left which characterized the inter-war period was viewed by liberal-minded people in Great Britain and the United States with

particular distaste, mainly because the individualist
Puritan tradition among the English-speaking peoples was far more powerful a force than in Europe
(where the opposition to institutional Christianity
took the form, almost exclusively, of a disruptive
and morally degenerate anti-clericalism); but also,
perhaps, because until 1945 the real danger to
Western civilization from Russia was not fully
appreciated by the Atlantic powers.

There was thus a widespread, and in the United
States a vociferous, welcome for Professor Toynbee,
when he stepped into the breach and rallied the
dispirited believers in progress with the doctrine of
challenge and response. He saw that what was
needed, if the situation was to be saved for the
progressives, was a theory of history which faced
the facts of cultural history, but by virtue of which
decline was a step on the upward path: just as, to
the economic planners, by reference to the law of
trial and error, error itself becomes synonymous
with progress.

Professor Toynbee's doctrine of challenge and
response is a dialectical view of history, which sees
each civilization offering a challenge to those outside
its orbit, and by this challenge engendering a re-

sponse and energizing the cultures with which it is in contact; until in time one of them becomes dominant, only to give way in the course of centuries before another response to its own challange —each civilization in turn playing the part of 'the priest who slew the slayer and shall himself be slain.' In this way it might seem that the objections to the simple theories of the Enlightenment and to the rigid determinism of Spengler were alike avoided, without any need to resort to the fallacies involved in applying an astronomical time scale to cultural history. But can history, in fact, be written in this way? Can civilizations, regions, and cultures be personified? Does not the practice involve an absolute falsification? Can any valid meaning be given in fact to such terms as 'the West' and 'the world'?

All decisive inventions, as Professor Toynbee himself admits, originate with individuals. The torch is handed on by individuals and it is extinguished or dimmed by other individuals. Is it not a monstrous error to assume that individuals, be they saints or sages, rulers or conquerors, are merely the unconscious instruments of societies or cultures or regions with an inherent dynamism of their own? And does it not make nonsense of a story which is plain enough to read, which tells us, in fact, why and in what respect the Christian civilization is as unique as it claims to be? Is there, indeed, any bone-structure in history to support the view that it is a constant clash of warring cultures? Let us look, for a change, at the facts.

THE earliest high city civilizations were in the temple-states of the mother goddess, static civilizations reflecting the outlook of the peasant culture. These temple-states were overthrown by successive invasions of fighting pastoralists, Jews, Hittites, and Indo-Europeans, whose sky-god personified the masculine and dynamic qualities also latent in human nature. But once the wandering dynamism of the pastoralist became acquainted with the peasant techniques and the use of metals, man, with his feet planted on the fertile earth but with his eyes on the stars, was equipped to start on the high adventure of history.

'I made the fortress of Egypt,' wrote Totmes I in the sixteenth century B.C., 'as far as the circuit of the sun.' It was a conscious personal act, as was that of Totmes III, when he destroyed the Syrian armies at the Battle of Megiddo. The decisive event was not the battle of armies but its sequel, perhaps the first, certainly the first successful, imposition of ordered government from a distance over an alien people. This was the discovery of a technique as decisive and as revolutionary as the change from food gathering to food cultivation. The assumption of jurisdiction by the conqueror, in place of the spoliation of the conquered, marked the beginning of political history.

With this discovery, the chief power in Asia Minor passed in turn to the Hittites, the Assyrians, the Babylonians, and the Persians, whose empire was overthrown by Alexander the Great at Gaugamela in 331 B.C. But for all its drama, is it historical to speak of that victory as the victory of the classical civilization, or indeed to distinguish, as Professor Toynbee does, between the civilization of Alexander and that of the armies which he defeated? The Greeks of the mainland had learnt their civilization from the Ionian cities, which had preserved their independence amid the clash of contending empires by virtue of sea power, the wealth derived from maritime enterprise, and the protection of the pow-

erful buffer state of Lydia. Not until Cyrus conquered Lydia in 546 B.C. were the Greeks brought
face to face with the organized forces of a great
land empire. The struggle of the Greek confederacy
against Persia marks the beginning of the political
history of Europe, just as the art, architecture, and
literature of Greece mark the beginnings of European secular culture. But it was a struggle within
the area where a high city civilization had existed
for much more than a thousand years; and the
Greek civilization was long past its highest level of
achievement when the military genius of Alexander
made a Greek, for a brief moment, master of the
civilized world.

According to Professor Toynbee, 'Alexander's
march across Asia made as revolutionary a change
in the balance of power in the world as the voyages
of da Gama and Columbus, and like them, it was
followed by wider conquests in later generations.'
It was, in fact, followed immediately by the death
of Alexander and the disruption of the area of his
conquests into four polyglot empires, none of which
survived, if we except Egypt, which again became
an independent kingdom, as it had been for countless generations before. Professor Toynbee turns the

trick by fusing the Greek and Roman worlds into one 'Graeco-Roman' culture and setting that culture on a march of conquest against Asia, Africa, and the rest of Europe. In justification, he remarks that the Greek of the New Testament, which, without acknowledgments to Mr. Ogden, he calls 'basic Greek,' was understood from Ceylon to the hinterland of Marseilles! Marseilles was certainly a Greek city, but it was not founded as the result of conquest. The Greek language had become the lingua franca of the Mediterranean world by virtue of the activities of the Greek merchants, not of the march of Greek armies. The same was true of the foundation of such other famous cities as Tarentum and Saguntum. The efforts of Athens and Sparta to unite and defend the Greek-speaking world were half-hearted and never long sustained. Able to defend their mainland and their home waters, the Greeks, for all their genius, had no aptitude for world government, and never attempted it. Their only great conqueror, Alexander, proclaimed a new gospel of his own, the brotherhood of all men without distinction of race, religion, or language: his self-imposed mission was, in plain fact, the reverse of a *kulturkampf*.

37

The Romans imposed on themselves a quite different mission, to impose peace, law, and security of communications by sea and land on that world of independent city states which long preceded the establishment of Roman rule. Marseilles was founded in 600 B.C., two and a half centuries before Alexander, and six centuries before the Roman Empire came into being. A call from Sicily for help led to the First Punic War; the Carthaginian siege of Saguntum led to the Second Punic War; a call for help from Massanissa, who had been attacked by Carthage in 150 B.C., led to the Third Punic War, and the destruction of Carthage. Similarly, the decisive Second Macedonian War began with an appeal to Rome by Pergamum, Rhodes, and Athens for protection from Antiochus of Syria. In the course of this and the subsequent Syrian and Third Macedonian Wars, Rome broke the power of Macedonia and Syria, and removed the threat of an oriental monarchy dominant over the cities of the eastern Mediterranean.

Even Gaul and Britain were civilized before, not after, they were conquered. Long before Caesar's time, the Celtic kingdoms beyond the indeterminate frontier of trans-Alpine Gaul had their cities, their coinage, and their political arrangements. The Celtic chieftains were largely Latin-speaking. They farmed intensively, and in the land of the Belgae, the present Picardy, the population before Caesar's time has been estimated at forty-two per square mile, a density greater than that of much of Scotland and Ireland to-day. Accounts of the high Celtic civilization have come down to us in the stories of Greek travellers in the second century B.C. Romanization was already in process in Britain before Caesar's abortive expedition, and proceeded by leaps and bounds after Caesar had come and gone. Strabo's account is conclusive. By the time of Claudius's invasion, the rulers of Southern Britain unquestionably spoke and wrote Latin, and they habitually drank Italian wine from Italian or Gaulish glassware. They used ornaments of Campanian silver or bronze, and wore clothes of linen, silk, and wool, perhaps imported from lands as distant as India. The population of south-east England was distinctly cosmopolitan. The trading community contained Gauls, Greeks, and Italians as well as the Celtic invaders. Only a slight resistance was offered the first invaders, and when the Emperor Claudius arrived he received the submission of sixteen kings in sixteen days. Yet Professor Toynbee tells us that the 'Graeco-Roman' civilization 'had been propagated by force of arms,' and, a little later, that the 'Greek and Roman dominant minority had devastated the world by conquering and plundering it and were now (in the second century A.D.) patrolling the ruins.'[1]

This picture of the military aggression and the racial exclusiveness of the 'Graeco-Roman' culture is essential to Professor Toynbee's rationalization of the historical process. If challenge and response is the key to the riddle of history, and the instrument of human progress, the fall of the Western Empire must represent, firstly, the ending of a challenge by a response, and secondly, a step on the upward path. So he tells how the brutal, aggressive, domi-

[1] A defender of Dr. Toynbee writing in the *Times Literary Supplement* of May 7th accused me of falsifying history in this passage. His argument was that I had not referred either to the slight resistance before Claudius arrived (I have now done so) or to the numerous rebellions which disturbed the country during the five centuries of Roman rule. I have no wish to represent the Romans as angels from on high, but the fact that, like the English monarchy between 1500 and 1920, they had to face numerous rebellions and invasions does not alter the fact that Romanization had preceded the conquest; it was not imposed by force of arms.

neering 'Graeco-Romans' fell victim to the rebellion of their Christian subjects. But is the story true? Did the world take its conquerors captive by converting them to new religions which made no discrimination 'between rulers and subjects, between Greeks, orientals, and barbarians'?

The central feature of the Roman world was not, in truth, military rule but civic autonomy protected by military frontiers. Moreover, there was no Latin 'dominance.' The citizenship had been given to all, irrespective of race or creeds, long before the end of the Western Empire. It was not Christianity which introduced non-discrimination to the world. Greeks, Syrians, Africans, Illyrians, and British all occupied the imperial throne in this world which Professor Toynbee so strangely describes as given to racial discrimination.

Secondly, the people who had been 'conquered' (though the word is not really admissible) by Rome were not the people who overthrew Rome. Professor Toynbee leads his readers to imagine the Roman Empire as a military empire, divided into Roman officers and soldiers with a Roman governing class, on the one side, and on the other, alien (Christian) subjects, who ultimately made their conquerors captive. This was not so. It was not only the emperors who were of all races and creeds, but the soldiery on the frontiers who, by the second century, were almost wholly, and by the third century, entirely, non-Roman. There were no racial or religious distinctions between 'rulers' and 'subjects.' The only distinction was between those who were citizens and those who were not, and in the Christian era this distinction had very largely ceased to be racial: it was never religious. The Empire was not overthrown by rebellion from within but by invasion from without. The barbarians broke the frontiers to get inside them. Periodically, for more than a century, the continuous pressure on the frontier had been eased by allowing advancing tribes to cross and settle within the frontiers. By the time the final crisis came, there was such a mixture of population within the Empire that the defeat of the legions and the over-running of the frontiers in the east meant little more than a change of government. City life and village life declined, naturally enough, with the decline of trade, but it never ceased except in Spain and Britain (the Christian Sees were continually occupied), and in Spain and Britain the collapse of civilization was only the indirect result of the ending of Roman rule. The invasions of the Moors and the Anglo-Saxons alike stemmed from centres outside the boundaries of the old empire. So long as the empire existed they never invaded it. It was the final collapse of Roman rule in Spain and Britain which provided the Moors and the Saxons with the opportunity for an easy conquest, but the fact that Britain (within two centuries) and Spain (progressively throughout some centuries) were brought back within the frontiers of Christian civilization was not due to the missionary zeal of the Christian conquerors of Rome, but to the survival of the framework of Roman Christianity, and the tradition of town life within the frontiers of the old Roman Empire. In other words, it was because the Roman Church and Church government survived elsewhere, and because the apostolic succession was elsewhere preserved, not because the secular empire of the West collapsed, that Christian civilization was preserved on the mainland of Europe, came back eventually to Britain and Spain, and spread to Germany.

Where then is the parallel which Professor Toynbee has asked us to see, in the story of the 'Graeco-Roman' world and its downfall, with the situation of our own civilization to-day? If, in fact, it was the collapse of the Roman world which rendered possible the brilliant flowering of our modern civilization four centuries later, then we might be tempted (although perhaps not beyond endurance) to share his conclusion about the present-day crisis. If, on the other hand, the real story is quite different, if Christian civilization survived (as we have suggested) to come to full fruition in the great Christian centuries, *in spite of* what was destroyed and *only because of* what was preserved from the pre-existing Roman world, not because the Roman Empire surrendered to the barbarians but because the Roman Church did not, we shall surely be right in reaching a very different conclusion from that suggested by Professor Toynbee.

THE Christian religion was not, either in form or content, one of a number of oriental religions; it was rooted in the historical present, in the fact of the Resurrection, the conclusive link in a chain of evidence about an historical person who proved himself, so his followers claimed and to-day still claim, to be the Son of God.

This central event in the history of mankind took place within, not without, the Roman world, and the message of Christ was carried to the heart of the empire and to the whole of the Greek world by a Greek-speaking Roman citizen. It was the fact that the hierarchical government of the Church, with its centralized administration and its defined creed, had already been roughly established throughout

the Roman world by the time of the barbarian
invasions, that enabled city life and the traditions of
civilized living to survive. Furthermore, it was this
fact which made inevitable the conversion of the
new rulers of the West, who had, if they were to
establish their authority, to make terms with a body
which not only claimed to hold the keys to the
kingdom of Heaven, and for this reason held the
allegiance of vast numbers in all lands; but which
was also the sole heir to the tradition of ordered
government, to the technique of administration, and
to the literary and artistic traditions of Greece and
Rome. It was the Roman Church which captured
its conquerors, not the victims of the Roman military conquest who conquered Rome. Such lesson
as is to be drawn (if any can be) from the remote
past is, therefore, precisely the opposite of that
which Professor Toynbee appears to draw, when
he asks us to remember the conversion of the imperial power of Rome, when faced by a challenge
from without, to the religion of its would-be conquerors. 'Is something like this,' he asks about our
own time and world, 'going to be written into the
unfinished history of the world's encounter with
the West?'

How this obscurely worded question must be interpreted is clear enough. 'The world' is the East, plus Russia, against which 'the West' has, Professor Toynbee tells us, been in a state of constant aggression 'for four or five hundred years.'

Is this 'aggression' of the modern 'West' at all less fanciful than the Professor's story of the 'Graeco-Romans' imposing their ideas by force on a reluctant world?

To begin the history of Western Christendom's encounters with its neighbours in the sixteenth century is, surely, to play ducks and drakes with history, but Professor Toynbee himself seems a little uncertain about his dates. On the first page of his book, 'the world' has been 'hit hard' by the West 'now for four or five hundred years.' This is repeated two paragraphs later. Three paragraphs later, however, we are told that the aggression of the West against Russia began in the thirteenth and fourteenth centuries, and a little later (on page 7) of the same first chapter that the threat to Russia from the West 'has been a constant threat from the thirteenth century till 1945.'

This is strange enough, but still more so the news of the recent aggressions of the West against Russia in 1941, 1914, 1812, and 1709. This last-named year was the date of the Battle of Poltava, an incident in a war of conquest started by Peter the Great which ended in the conquest by Russia of Livonia and Esthonia, among other territories, and also of a number of Baltic islands; and which destroyed for ever the continental power of Sweden. And in what sense that is rational can Hitler's attack on Russia be termed the aggression of the West: in which case the peoples of Great Britain, France, Belgium, Holland, Scandinavia, and the United States must be reckoned as outside the Western fold? And was Russia's mobilization against Germany in 1914 an act of Western aggression? The history of Russia from 1480 to the present day has, as we have seen, been the history of a steady and unparalleled expansion, marked by only one set-back in 1918, when she was forced to restore Poland to the Poles and to give independence to the Baltic republics and Finland. To represent this vast imperial adventure as a series of *revanches* against persistent aggressions from the West over four or five or seven centuries, is quite misleading.

To make any sense at all it is necessary to assume that 'the West,' instead of being, as it is, a term to which historians must give through the centuries a whole series of different connotations, is a sentient and purposeful organism, or at least an organism stirred every century or so by a recurrent urge to move eastward. It is to make of history one of those chronicle plays where we see the adolescent, the man at the height of his powers, and, finally, the same man in his old age, and are asked to see in a series of incidents, separated by intervals of twenty years or so, the same vices and virtues persistently at work, imposing a recurring pattern on the events of his life. Such a treatment of the historical process is highly speculative even when it is applied to a unitary state, with a highly organized governing machine which can be assumed to be, over a long period of time, the devisor as well as the executant of policy. Even then, the treatment is valid only within narrow limits. There is a sense in which we can say, for instance, that both the German General Staff and the Russian Foreign Office have pursued a fairly steady policy over the last one hundred years, but it would be quite untrue to say the same of all those individuals who have directed these organizations, or of the sovereigns whom they have served.

The West, however, has never had one government even in Europe except during the first four centuries of the Christian era, and it is only with the Church in mind that we can speak of the Western world as a continuing entity after the fall of the Western Empire. Politically speaking, it is possible to attribute a common policy to the West before the present decade only in speaking of the early crusades, and in relation to the limited objectives there pursued. It is possible, although it is mere speculation, that the empire of Charlemagne might have consolidated itself into a unitary system of government for western continental Europe, but for the centrifugal pull on the Frankish frontiers from the Scandinavian and Eastern invaders. Professor Toynbee, however, ignores the long and bitter struggle of Europe against her invaders. He presents a picture of strong and unified Graeco-Roman (later, a Mediaeval Christian) society pressing eastward. Our history books, still the most reliable guides in these matters, have quite a different story to tell. From the time of Marathon and Salamis, in

the fifth century B.C., down to the defeat of the
Turks before Vienna in 1683, the high civilization
of Europe, centred round the Mediterranean basin,
has been under almost continual pressure from the
North-east and the East.

First, the Persians and their allies sought to
overwhelm the Greek world. Then, Rome had to
face the successive challenge of the Phoenicians
from Carthage, of the Parthians, and, finally, of the
successive waves of Gothic and Visigothic invaders
from the East and North-East. These invaders first
threatened the fortified frontiers in 220, occupied
Dacia in 257, and inflicted a decisive military defeat on the Romans at Adrianople in 378 B.C.

It is perhaps natural for the contemporary
English-speaking world, most of it to-day separated
from Europe by thousands of miles of ocean, and
mostly descended from ancestors who lived only on
the very fringes of the Graeco-Roman world, to see
the Greeks and Romans themselves as alien conquerors. Indeed, this view has been to some extent
fixed in the popular mind by the Reformation,
which has taught so many in the English-speaking
world to regard not only the peoples of the Mediterranean basin, but their culture, as something

alien which has impinged upon, and even, some would say, corrupted, a purer nordic version. That was Hitler's view, but it is none the less a lie.

Our civilization is rooted in the Graeco-Roman culture and the Christian revelation. The towns which bred the one and the church which taught and preserved the other, were alike protected for five vital centuries by the defensive military frontiers of the Roman republic and Empire, which held out against successive waves of oriental or barbarian invaders. The physical remains of their great defensive works can be seen in Hadrian's Wall in the north of England, and in the even more formidable works, fifty feet thick and twelve feet high, which still stand in the Dobrudja. These vast undertakings were continuously manned for some centuries by tens of thousands of legionaries and bear vivid witness, not to a habit of aggression, but to a determined and unparalleled energy of systematic and prepared defence against almost continuous aggression from without. We may think to-day of Marcus Aurelius as a meditative philosopher, but he and his successors spent most of their life in the field, fighting the barbarians from the North-East. When, in the fifth century, the defences of the West were at last over-run, the invaders were themselves, by then, Latin speaking, just as the leaders of the imperial forces were themselves, and had been for many decades, Romanized Goths, Spaniards and Africans.

From the resulting Gothic and Visigothic kingdoms modern Europe was born, but it was a slow and anxious process of growth, and the idea of Europe in this early Gothic twilight as an aggressor against the East, is, as near as may be, the exact opposite of the truth.

Long before Western Europe could be said to have taken any political shape, the Goths had to face the challenge of the Huns under Attila, and the defeat of the Huns at Chalons in 461 was one of the decisive battles of the world. The Anglo-Saxons were, at the same time, invading Britain, which, for a time, was wholly lost to the civilized world. The defeat of Attila provided a temporary lull in Europe, but it was not long before the Moors provided yet another great challenge from the East to the West—the sixth since the Battle of Marathon. This challenge was held on the line of the Pyrenees, after the Moorish invaders had been thrown out of France by Charles Martel in 732, but

Spain was lost to Europe for some centuries, and only finally united under Christian sovereignty in 1492. Meanwhile a fresh peril, but not, for once, from the East, threatened what had become, in 800 A.D., the new Empire of the West. This was the Viking invasion. The pressure on France was continuous through the ninth and tenth centuries. Simultaneously the eastern frontiers were under constant threat from the Magyars and the Wends. The threat to the eastern frontier of Europe remained acute until 955 when the Emperor, Otto the Great, defeated the Magyars at the river Lech (in a battle perhaps as decisive as Marathon and Chalons),[1] and the Wends in the Mechlenburg marshes. Barely ten years later the frontier was again over-run, settlements at Havelburg and Brandenburg were wiped out, and Hamburg was laid in ruins. This blow was repaired; the frontier was restored; but for centuries it had to be held by force and was never firmly secured. Beyond the line of the Elbe, in the Middle Ages as to-day, the organization of Christendom was shadowy.

Whether, but for the prolonged strain to which the territories now forming France, Spain and

[1] R. W. Southern, *Making of the Middle Ages*.

54

England were put by the Viking invasions of the ninth and tenth centuries, the new Empire might have consolidated its political organization and military strength and entered upon a campaign of aggression against the East we cannot say. We can say that, given the situation as it actually was, Europe was thrown inevitably on the defensive, and so remained, until Napoleon invaded Russia in 1812, not as the representative and leader of the West, let alone of Christian civilization, but as the heir to a revolution against Western traditions and the declared enemy of the rest of Europe, seeking in the dream of a Russian conquest the means not to impose Europe on the East, but to impose the revolution on Europe.

Between the time of Charlemagne and the time of Napoleon's invasion of Rome lies a span of exactly a thousand years, a period marked not by Christian-Graeco-Roman aggression but by the strong and almost continuous pressure against the eastern frontier of western Christendom by the Moslem, the Mongol, the Slav and the Magyar.[1]

[1] "A Mongolian race who slipped into the empty Pannonian plain, dividing the northern from the southern Slavs"—H. A. L. Fisher, *A History of Europe*, Vol. I, p. 193.

The Moslem conquest of North Africa began in
670. In the ninth century began the domination
of the Mediterranean itself. Crete was captured in
826, Sicily invaded in 877 and its conquest com-
pleted in 902. By the end of the tenth century the
Mediterranean was a Moslem lake. In the same
century, as we have seen, the great struggle of the
West with the Magyars and the Wends reached a
crisis. Only barely, and after a series of desperate
struggles, were the outposts of Christendom main-
tained beyond the Elbe. Meanwhile the Moslem
invaders had reached Italy. In 1004 they sacked
Pisa, in 1009 they captured the Holy Sepulchre at
Jerusalem, in 1011 they sacked Pisa again, and in
1018 they captured Sardinia.

And now Christendom was to be subjected
to a new and fiercer attack. From his base in
Afghanistan, Mahmoud, the first of the great
Turkish conquerors, started, at the turn of the
eleventh century, on his career of conquest, which
gave him an empire which stretched from Ispahan
to Lahore. In 1055 the second great Turkish conqueror, Tughril Bey, became the secular ruler of all
Islam, conquered Syria and Jerusalem, and defeated the Byzantine Emperor at Manzikert in

1071. Here Professor Toynbee's admirers can breathe a short sigh of relief, for here, after one thousand four hundred years of eastern aggression, we find the first faint counter-move of the West, not in the form of an effort at military or political conquest, but in the form of the first Crusade—a shocking action, we are asked to believe, but, in fact, merely a disinterested effort (unlike some of the later Crusades) to rescue the holy places of Palestine from Moslem domination and preserve them as shrines for Christian pilgrims. Alas! for Professor Toynbee's theory; the 'aggressors' were only temporarily successful. The Latin kingdom of Jerusalem did not endure. The Christian holy places did not remain in Christian hands, but in the hands of the bold invaders from Afghanistan, who proceeded, at no distant date, to attempt the conquest of Southeastern Europe.

The Turks had to face rival eastern aggressors in the shape of the Mongols under Genghis Khan, who conquered Samarkand, Bokhara and Persia between 1218 and 1224. Next the Mongols defeated the Russians and captured Moscow, and proceeded to invade Poland and Hungary in 1241. These great conquerors (about whom the learned

57

Professor is strangely silent) moved East as well as West and conquered and ruled in China from 1279 to 1378. Meanwhile 'aggressive' Westerners had been thrown back from their one Asiatic outpost in Palestine. The loss of Acre in 1291 marked the end of Christian rule in the Near East. The Crusades had failed not for lack of faith but for lack of military force. The Eastern offensive continued.

In 1356, Suleiman, the Turkish Sultan, marched into Europe and founded on the Gallipoli peninsula the first Turkish settlement on European soil. A little later Adrianople became the Turkish capital, and by the end of the century the Turkish frontiers had reached the Danube. In 1382 the Turks captured Sofia. In 1422 came the first siege of Constantinople; after the fall of Constantinople in 1453 the Turkish expansion into Eastern Europe became rapid—Greece, Serbia, Bosnia and Herzogovinia all fell to the oriental invaders within ten years. These conquests held for centuries, and in the sixteenth century the Turkish power reached its height during the reign of Suleyman the Magnificent (1520-1566). The defeat of Hungary on the historic field of Mohacs in 1526, following, as it did, on the capture of Belgrade and the capitulation of Rhodes, sealed the doom of Hungary as an independent kingdom, and withdrew the frontiers of Christendom to the gates of Vienna.

Submitted to various and constant pressures from the East, the Poles and the Magyars had never been able either to create a stable national government for themselves or to find a basis for co-operation with each other in the defence of the West. The result was the permanent establishment of Turkish dominance in South-East Europe and the isolation of Poland between the Habsburg and the Romanoff empires. But the Habsburg empire was itself a defensive organization called into effective being as "the only valid bulwark against a great and aggressive Moslem Empire."[1] The Austrian Empire was and remained, by reason alike of its origin and its composition, incapable of aggression. In fact, as late as 1683, the Turks again reached the gates of Vienna, only to be thrown back by the combined efforts of Austrians and Poles.

Professor Toynbee speaks of none of these things.

It is, to say the least of it, an unfortunate moment that he has chosen for silence, when the Christian world is once again threatened with ag-

[1] H. A. L. Fisher, *A History of Europe,* Vol. 1, p. 497.

gression from the East and when, once again, it can only be saved by an energetic, systematic, prepared defensive which only the persistent enemies of our civilization will dare to call aggression.

Indeed, we learn from Professor Toynbee nothing of the long and bitter struggle of Europe against her invaders, but only of the Moslem invasions of the seventh century marking the beginning of the 'liberation' of the world from 'Christian-Graeco-Roman dominance.' Coming swiftly from that point to the sixteenth century, he records how 'the Western world's retort to the conquest of Eastern Orthodox Christianity in the fourteenth and fifteenth centuries had not been to make a fresh frontal attack on the Islamic world . . . but to encircle Islam by conquering the ocean'; and how the transit of the oceans by the Spaniards 'opened up in the Philippine Islands a new East Asian frontier' between Western Christendom and Islam. It is a fascinating story, but is it history?

After this first exercise in global strategy, the West, according to Professor Toynbee, continued its persistent aggression against Russia, but kept, at the same time, an eye on Islam. The military efforts of the West were greatly assisted by successive technological revolutions which, in varying degrees, forced westernization not only on Russia (Peter the Great) and Turkey (the Young Turks, and later, and more efficiently, Mustapha Kemal), but also on Japan and on Egypt.

By and large, does this picture make sense? Professor Toynbee rightly points out that there is widespread unrest throughout Asia and Africa to-day, and a great deal of hostility to the Western powers. But was westernization, in fact, forced on the East, and still more relevantly, was it forced at the point of a bayonet? And is it true that the only doctrine we have given to the East is nationalism, and that the only skills are technological? Are there no Christians in Asia or Africa? And are there no liberals and no humanists? Are the Indians, the Pakistanis, and the Africans asking to be allowed to revert to some other antecedent way of life and thought; or are they asking to be allowed, and being allowed, to build higher and faster on the foundation of those freedoms of conscience, of thought, of expression, of association, and of worship, which they have learnt from the West? And has China,[1] still enslaved, been chiefly the victim of Western or of Eastern aggression? And is not trade rather than war the main 'westernizing' influence? And does trade follow the flag or does it, as Sir Stanley Unwin is so fond of saying, follow the book? Finally, is that higher material standard of life which is associated with international trade and city life really a 'Western' way of life? Is it not as old as civilization itself, which began most certainly in the East and not in the West? Is not the whole dichotomy between East and West, on the long view which Professor Toynbee asks us to take, wholly unsound?

Nothing is stranger than the obsession of liberal humanists with military power. They detect its influence everywhere but they ignore its origins and greatly exaggerate its consequences. The motive force behind the successive stages of westernization of Russia and Turkey was the determination of

[1] Professor Toynbee is a greater authority on China than the present writer, but it can surely be fairly argued that until 1946 China presented the classic instance of a society absorbing what it wanted of an alien culture without being subjected to any loss of political, cultural or religious independence. To describe China as a victim of *Western* aggression seems, therefore, to say the least of it, a wild over-statement.

Russian and Turkish usurpers, adventurers, and revolutionaries to consolidate the personal power which they had seized or wished to extend. Precisely the same cause led to the creation of the first national army—the French army of the Revolution forged into a great fighting instrument by the military genius of a Corsican adventurer. To give a unity and dialectical significance to these historical accidents we had to be given the story of the prolonged and continuous military aggression of the West, which brought into action against it armies forced to equip themselves (the Russians sooner, the Turks much later) with Western weapons. But neither the challenge nor the response is historically true. Nothing better illustrates the curiosities of Professor Toynbee's method than his assumption that the Young Turks movement came from the study of Western military text-books by young military officers. It might have done so, perhaps, although history has yet to record a successful subalterns' revolution, but was it so in fact? Professor Toynbee has much to say of Enver, who was certainly a young officer, but his fellow conspirators were Talaat, a civil servant in Salonica, and Djavid, a Jewish financier. The secret society, the Com-

mittee of Union and Progress, which created the
revolution, met first at Geneva, when it was in
touch with Russian revolutionaries; and it was from
them, not from Vickers or the *Comité des Forges,*
still less from West Point, Camberley, or St. Cyr,
that these adventurers learnt the technique of seiz-
ing power by force. The members of the committee
were not, in the main, young officers (though there
were a number of these), but the intelligentsia of
the outlying Turkish seaport towns, mainly doctors
and lawyers with a strong Jewish element. The importance of the 1908 revolution was that it was the
first successful revolution in modern history made
by professional revolutionaries. It was not the
product of a response to Western aggression; it was
neither a national nor an Asiatic reaction to the
pressure of outside forces; it was the characteristic
product of Western civilization cut off from its
Christian roots: of the printing press, secular education, irreligion, and untrammelled ambition—in
short, of a world determined on freedom outside a
closed moral system.

A similar doubt is aroused by Professor Toynbee's
account of the Russian victory in 1945, which (by
way of contrast with their defeat in 1917, which

was due, we are told, to 'industrial Western technology') is attributed to the Communist technological revolution. Is either statement really true? The decisive event for Russia in the 1914–17 war was the failure of the campaign in East Prussia in August and September 1914—a failure as decisive as Moltke's failure on the Marne. This defeat was due neither to shortage of men nor to inferior equipment; it was due to criminally bad generalship and non-existent staff work. On a long view, the whole series of defeats suffered by the Russian armies in World War I was due to misgovernment, not to inferiority in material. As to the Russian 'victory' over the Germans, how much of the allied victory of 1945 was due to Russian technology and how much to the American and British armies, navies, and air forces? Without the aid of their Western and Christian allies, is it to be doubted for a moment that Russia would have been totally defeated?

And is Professor Toynbee any surer a guide when he leaves military for political history? Is a 'Western spiritual weapon' a historically accurate description of the mainspring of Russia's power to-day? And is it true that in the present encounter between

Russia and the West, 'the spiritual initiative . . . has now passed, *at any rate for the moment,* from the Western to the Russian side'? Those words which I have italicized made one reader, at any rate, gasp![1]

---

[1] Professor Toynbee has since explained (the *Times Literary Supplement,* April 16th) his extraordinary reference to the Russian spiritual initiative by saying that 'Communism has overtrumped our little idol *homunculus* by setting up a big idol—*Leviathan-Juggernaut,* the apotheosis of collective human power—which is a less unworthy human object of devotion than freedom for secular private enterprise.' I still gasp. Professor Toynbee here is not content to query the truth of Christianity as held to-day, but seems to ignore its very existence.

IT is not possible, of course, for a Christian to be a theoretical Communist, because Communism, of its essence, makes the family subordinate to the State, makes man a function of the machine, and denies to the family that element of economic independence and free choice which is necessary if men and women are to be free moral agents. To that point we shall return. For a non-Christian, however, it is admittedly possible to hold sincerely that the Communist pattern of society is the ideal. But is it possible for anyone not wholly indifferent to all natural virtue to regard the present Russian effort to impose her regime on the world as an effort so markedly spiritual in character as to place the entire Christian world at a spiritual disadvantage? Do they blush in the Vatican for

shame at their own failings when they consider the
lofty moral standards held sacrosanct in the Kremlin? Do the fellows of All Souls fall silent over their
port in self-abasement as they contemplate the spec-
tacle of a society in Russia devoted to the selfless
pursuit of the good, the beautiful, and the true?
These questions are addressed not only to Christians, but also to the liberal humanist world to
which Professor Toynbee is heir and for which he
is spokesman.

Finally let us ask ourselves what is the Professor's
attitude to Communism, as such.

'Communism,' he writes, 'seems to the great
majority of people in the West to be a perverse,
misguided, and disastrous doctrine and way of life.
A theologian might put it that our great modern
Western heresiarch Karl Marx has made what is a
heretic's characteristic intellectual mistake and
moral aberration. In putting his finger on one point
in orthodox practice in which there has been a
crying need for reform, he has lost sight of all other
considerations and therefore has produced a remedy
that is worse than the disease.

'The Russians' recent success in capturing the
initiative from us . . . does not, of course, mean that

Communism is destined to prevail. . . . All the same, Communism's success, so far as it has gone, looks like a portent of things to come. What it does tell us is that the present encounter between the world and the West is now moving off the technological plane on to the spiritual plane.'

There are some curious features in these paragraphs. First, Dr. Toynbee, in his lectures, very carefully refrained from expressing his own opinion, which, however, he has since been at great pains to make clear. He neither expects nor desires the triumph of Communism. Nevertheless, he congratulates the Communist on putting his finger on one point (in our Western civilization) where there is a 'crying need for reform.' By implication, this must mean a point which the West itself has not tried, at least effectively, to reform.

It would have been natural in a series of lectures addressed to millions of listeners, and later to be reprinted *in extenso* in two continents, for the writer to make clear what was the crying scandal on which the kindly reforming Communist had put his finger. Manifestly it is not our humanitarianism, our keen devotion to the cause of personal freedom or political self-government, or our vast experiments in social reform or public health services. What is it then that we in the West have left undone which has been done in Russia, unless it is the supreme concentration of economic, and therefore of political, power in the hands of an infinitesimal minority, with the professed object of more effectively providing, equally for all, their material needs, by the denial of economic, and therefore of political and moral, freedom.

This cannot be what is meant, because if it were, we should be being asked to infer that the one good thing about the Communists is Communism. The mystery remains.

If we value our skins, let alone our souls, these professorial obscurities are not to our peace. The purpose of the pattern imposed, not by the global strategists of 'the West,' or 'the Christian-Graeco-Roman culture' planning their aggressions down the centuries, but by Professor Toynbee himself, is all too clear. First of all, just as we are asked to see the Roman Empire in the second century A.D. menaced by a number of new religions, so to-day we are asked to see our rootless, faithless, Western world challenged by the faith of India and China, and by that well-known 'Christian heresy' associated with the name of Karl Marx. Our world, we are to infer, has so completely lost its faith in Christianity that it is really only a question of what shall take its place. 'The Western world reacted to this disillusioning, self-inflicted experience of the evils of religious fanaticism' (the Wars of Religion) 'by withdrawing its treasure from religion and reinvesting it in technology.' Since then, Western civilization has gone 'like wildfire round the world' but now its course is run. This line of attack is, of course, familiar to Christian historians. We need not argue, say our enemies, as to the merits of Christian ethics or the truth of Christian dogma, because, perhaps unfortunately, no one either practises the one or believes in the other to-day.

In this way, Professor Toynbee frees himself, as he thinks, from the necessity of examining the Christian case. It is with our own contemporary, post-Christian civilization that he is alone concerned. This civilization, like all its predecessors, has had its hour of triumph and is now challenged. By comparison with a Christianity which has disintegrated into technology, Communism is a spiritual creed. The West has lost its spiritual initiative.

This misdescription of our contemporary Western

civilization must be explicitly challenged. True it is, as Mallock[1] prophesied, that 'upon our generation, as upon that of Rome, calamity has at last fallen. . . . We have to-day real power in the hands of real ignorance, and the result has been not reorganization but ruin.' But those whom Mallock was attacking were not the main body of European and American citizens, but a rootless, sceptical minority of intellectuals claiming the right in the name of the latest new philosophy to lead mankind along new paths. This they have now done, and the ruin is visible to all. Furthermore, the new logicians are seeking to carry the work of distintegration further with the point-blank denial of the validity of value judgments. By proclaiming a sceptical nihilism as the representative thought of our times they assert what they wish to prove. Long ago they claimed to have destroyed the throne and the altar, to have blunted the edge of the two swords, to have abolished God and Caesar. Now they claim to have destroyed man himself, by destroying his belief in those values which can alone give dignity to his life and potency to his acts.

[1] *Is Life Worth Living?* by W. H. Mallock. Chatto & Windus, 1903.

The Lie About the West

But is the claim justified? Twice now in our lifetime the West has risen in its own defence against those who in the name of false gods called for surrender. In each case the challenge came from those who claimed to be able to create a better way of life for men subordinated to a superior governing instrument, and denied the right to organize their own community and to live their own lives in accordance with their own standards of freedom, honour, and justice. After the First World War, we had to face from the sceptics the strong challenge which twenty-five years ago I called 'The Lie about the War.' To-day, after the Second World War and at the height of the third (cold) war, we have a stronger challenge in the lie about the West. At bottom both are the same lie—that there was and is nothing in our way of life which is much better or worse than any other; that we were and are to-day drawn into a false struggle on immaterial issues by men intent only on seeking or retaining power; and that the finer souls and clearer minds have seen it all along and have had no heart for the fight. It was in the twenties the declared aim of these heroes of peace to educate a generation of men 'who would shudder at the sight of a rifle.' Had they succeeded in their aim, their children would have had ample opportunity for exercising the peculiar talent which such an education was to foster. The lie about the war collapsed in the face of the answer of the men who had fought the war. It was simply untrue that the finest minds and the purest souls of the 1914 generation were those who had stayed at home, or who had fought half-heartedly and with no belief in their cause. But although the lie was without justification it was not without some excuse. Many of the values for which we had fought had been betrayed. Many of those who had fought for them had themselves been left by their betrayers to starve in the gutter.

To-day there is no excuse.

We have seen in Germany and in Russia exactly why we must defend our institutions; we have seen the absolute corruption which comes from the absolute power of the State; we have seen the absolute dependence and abasement which is the lot of men who allow the family to be subordinated to the State and themselves to become functions of the machine. Worst of all, we have seen the moral degradation of once simple and decent people when a readiness to abrogate all human rights becomes

74

the only passport to a secure place in the hierarchy of the State. And how have these iniquities come to pass, and why there and not here? Because the dignity that came to man with the Christian revelation, the dignity of man redeemed by Christ upon the Cross, has gone from him in those societies which have turned their backs on Christianity, which have uprooted the institutions necessary to the fortification of human weakness, and removed the incentive necessary to the practice of natural virtue; and which, in denying to man that political and economic independence necessary if he is to be a free moral agent, have checked at the very source his spiritual growth.

In the Western world none of these things has happened, but there are those who desire that they should, who wish to see our society as something post-Christian, something without sanctions, something empirical, the plaything of an evolutionary process in which power will come in full measure only to the destroyers of our traditional faith. And on this last point they are right. For the strength of the West does not lie in the academies but in the homes of the people. It is from them that the answer will come, provided the homes survive. Let us see to it that they do, but Professor Toynbee's book will not help. His lame and sceptical conclusions must tend to bring ever nearer that grim, bleak world foreseen by G. K. Chesterton, where

> Those who once to harvest home would come
> Hope for no harvest and possess no home.

That, at least, seems the most likely consequence of this strange rewriting of history, by which first the 'Graeco-Romans,' and then the Christians, are represented as bloodthirsty aggressors with their hands always on the sword, fighting their way forward across the pages of history: each in turn abandoning all pretence of belief in their professed creed and descending into the abyss—brute force or 'technology' their only weapon—and succumbing, or destined to succumb, to those who still have their eyes on higher things. This book, to be plain, reads as if it were intended to weaken our faith in western Christian civilization, and must, unless it is challenged, inevitably have that effect.

> *Non tali auxilio nec defensoribus istis*
> *Tempus eget.*

Never was a conclusion so abject reached by logic so defective.

LET us consider first the spiritual initiative which, 'for the moment at any rate,' has passed from the Christians to the Kremlin. We understand the initiative. They shoot first. Where, in heaven's name, is the spirituality? For let us be clear on this, he does not concede the spiritual initiative to British or American Communist theorists; he concedes it specifically to Russia. What are they offering to the world at the price of murder, economic slavery, and political oppression on a scale unknown in human history, these men between whom and ourselves (according to Professor Toynbee) the differences are so minute that they 'fade almost out of view' by contrast with those which separate us from the Indians or the Chinese? Let us put this also to the test of concrete illustration. Is it really true that when Pope Pius

XII greets his Indian or his Chinese cardinals, archbishops, and bishops he feels a wide, unbridgeable gulf and sighs for the comforting presence of M. Molotov or M. Vishinsky? Is it true that when Sir Winston Churchill has to talk to his fellow old-Harrovian, Mr. Nehru, he is similarly embarrassed? Does each of these great men in the secrecy of his heart say: 'If only it were Stalin, or Malenkov, whom I have to meet, then we should be talking the same language'?

What rubbish it all is!

But it is worse than that, for it is not 1917, when, to quite a large number of deluded professors, Lenin's gospel really seemed to hold out hope of a Utopia for the Russian working class, nor a hundred years hence when perhaps this pitiful martyrdom of half a continent may have drawn to its close. No! It is this very moment, when the firing-squads are busy from Prague to Vladivostok, when the total of political prisoners in the slave camps is higher than ever before—nearly twenty million souls—when the tide of murder in China is rising to heights never attained even in the tragic years of the so-called liberal revolution: it is now that we are asked in the name of English liberalism to greet the Katyn murderers as men indistinguishable from us in their ideals, only more spiritually minded in pursuit of them. Is it really sufficient to dismiss this as a mere verbal extravagance?

Our deep and passionate quarrel with the Communist society, as with the National Socialist society, is not, and never has been, political; it concerns precisely those things born of Christianity which are still recognized by all men of goodwill as necessary to the good life and the healthy society. Christian civilization is not just one among many; it is, and the world to-day provides overwhelming evidence of the fact, the only civilization built on the rights of the human personality, rights which derive from the belief in the immortality of the soul of man.

So wholly is our thought, our tradition, and our language Christian, that we tend to take for granted what in fact is a revolutionary conception. The doctrines of man's fall and redemption, of the equality of all men before God, of the ability and the obligation to win salvation, and consequently of the sanctity, dignity, and responsibility of the individual personality—these doctrines changed the face of the world. They gave a wholly new direction to human activity and necessitated a revolution

79

both in politics and morals. The 'rights' which are deducible from these doctrines are to-day universally recognized by all who are heirs to the tradition of Western European civilization, even by those who deny in whole or in part the doctrines themselves, and who lack the faith which inspired their remote ancestors to the task of building the first free civilization known to history.

It is not to democratic politicians, but to the belief in the primacy of the spiritual in the world order that all our freedoms, including that particular form of freedom known as democracy, are due. 'What shall it profit a man, if he shall gain the whole world, and lose his own soul?' Yet also: 'Render unto Caesar the things which are Caesar's.'

It was the doctrine implicit in these tremendous sayings which conquered the Eastern and Western Empires and determined the course of secular history almost to our own day. It was a revolution in thought which necessitated a revolution in institutions and, most notably and decisively for human freedom, the recognition of the distinction between Church and State. From the first, and with varying emphasis throughout the first twelve centuries of the Christian era, the Church was subject to attack from both sides. The long battle with Manichaeism and Gnosticism reflected the revolt of the Eastern mind from a religion which accepted the world as its platform; the repeated challenges of the later centuries to the increasing influence of the Church in secular affairs reflected the revolt of the Western mind, heir to the classical tradition, against a religion which sought to impose upon the world its own teleology.

It accords with the view of those who hold that the Divine revelation is a living thing, and therefore progressive in its operation, that the institutional complement to the Christian doctrine should have been worked out over several centuries. The oriental tradition, almost all-powerful at first in the Eastern Church, and finding its extreme expression in the exaggerated asceticism of the monks of the desert, for whom the world had no existence, is reflected even in St. Augustine's *Civitas Dei,* which borrowed the Roman term but not the Roman idea. Augustine's city is not a social organization directed to the service of God, but a fellowship of souls. Yet Augustine was one of the leaders in the fight against neo-Platonism and Manichaeism. His controversial writings proclaim insistently that every work of God is good, that creation therefore is not evil, and that the only source of evil is the creatures' misuse of their liberty. It was his life's work to begin the adaptation of the intellectual heritage of the ancient world to the purposes of the religion of Christ, and it was his fate and fortune to do so just when the Church in the West became the political heir of the Roman Empire. The defeat of Gnosticism and Manichaeism marked one stage in the process of definition, the necessity of seeking salvation through the world and its works. On this foundation, buttressed by the Augustinian doctrine of Grace, the Western Church proceeded to define in the course of the succeeding centuries the things which were Caesar's and the things which were not. Thus was brought back into the world the principle of secular authority subject to the moral law, a principle which proclaimed each man to belong to two states: a terrestrial state whose end is the common temporal good, and the universal state of the Church, whose end is eternal life.

Thus Christianity found a place for both man and God in the order of nature.

The contemporary enemies of our civilization are aware of these fundamental truths; they have realized all too clearly that it is Christian belief, and the institutions and the political philosophy which derive from this belief, which stands for ever as an obstacle to the realization of the tyrant's dream, the assertion of the absolute right of the State to command the actions and thoughts, and to dispose of the lives, of its citizens.

To the claim of the State to omnicompetence, only the Christian religion which Professor Toynbee tells us we have jettisoned has ever provided an answer. The civilization to which our religion has given birth is therefore, in fact as well as in theory, unique. It represents a practical achievement to which hundreds of millions of human beings have owed, and still to-day owe, the fact of freedom. That that freedom has always been imperfectly realized is due to the inherent imperfection of man. That the battle for freedom has been fought from generation to generation and that it is still being fought, is due to the unquenchable vitality of the gospel of Christ. Whatever the Professor may say, the Christian world still rests confidently on the promise made by Christ to His Church that the gates of hell shall not prevail against it. Secure in the knowledge of that promise we shall continue in faith, in hope, and also with charity, but none the less uncompromisingly, to fight for the freedom of mankind.

Nothing that has been said here in criticism of Professor Toynbee's thesis need or should be taken to imply that individual nations in the West, however defined, have never been guilty of aggression against the East. Nothing here written is, for instance, incompatible with the view that British imperialism, in its eighteenth- and nineteenth-century forms, is to be condemned. It is, indeed, often condemned by liberal opinion on both sides of the Atlantic. It is not the view of the present writer that this condemnation is justified: it could, I believe, be shown fairly easily that imperialism, by which is meant the imposition of an alien jurisdiction for longer or shorter periods over backward peoples, or over territories fallen into anarchy, is a policy which has been imposed by circumstance on all great powers, Eastern more often than Western, throughout recorded time. The difference between Eastern and Western imperialism has usually been found in the far greater respect for human rights of those imperial powers who were faithful to the Western Christian tradition, and in their readiness to grant to subject peoples the opportunity of fitting themselves for self-government and, eventually, for independence. This assuredly is very far from being the whole story, but the fact that much has been done in the past which would be regarded as unjustifiable, or worse, to-day, is proof of the vitality of those Western Christian values which are to-day challenged, not of their decay. The more we cherish these values, the more clearly we must recognize the failure of all societies at all times to live up to them. It remains, in my submission, as unhistorical to say that the effort to assert these values in the past has, on balance, been productive of anything but good for mankind, as it would be unethical to suggest that our efforts to defend these values should now be abandoned.

THIS BOOK MAY BE KEPT

14 Days

and may be renewed if not called for by
someone else.
A fine of 2¢ per day is charged if the book
is kept after the last date stamped below.

DUE	DUE	DUE